SUGAR GROVE PUBLIC LIBRARY DISTRICT
54 Snow Street / P.O. Box 1049
Sugar Grove, IL 60554
(630) 466-4686

W9-BVU-371

10/2/06

www.sugargrove.lib.il.us

SUGAR GROVE PUBLIC LIBRARY DISTRICT
54 Snow Street/P.O. Box 1049
Sugar Grove, IL 60554
(630) 466-4686

Rookie
Read-About® Math

A 3-D Birthday Party

Sugar Grove Public Library
54 Snow St.
Sugar Grove, IL 60554

DISCARDED

By Ellen B. Senisi

Subject Consultant
Chalice Bennett
Elementary Specialist
Martin Luther King Jr. Laboratory School
Evanston, Illinois

Reading Consultant
Cecilia Minden–Cupp, PhD
Former Director, Language and Literacy Program
Harvard Graduate School of Education

Children's Press®
A Division of Scholastic Inc.
New York   Toronto   London   Auckland   Sydney
Mexico City   New Delhi   Hong Kong
Danbury, Connecticut

Designer: Herman Adler Design
Photo Researcher: Caroline Anderson
The photo on the cover shows a boy holding a present at a birthday party.

Library of Congress Cataloging-in-Publication Data

Senisi, Ellen B.
  A 3-D birthday party / by Ellen Senisi.
      p. cm. — (Rookie read-about math)
  Includes index.
  ISBN-10: 0-516-29828-3 (lib. bdg.)   0-516-29849-6 (pbk.)
  ISBN-13: 978-0-516-29828-3 (lib. bdg.)   978-0-516-29849-8 (pbk.)
  1. Geometry, Solid—Juvenile literature. 2. Shapes—Juvenile literature.
3. Dimensional analysis—Juvenile literature. I. Title: Three-dimensional
birthday party. II. Title. III. Series.
  QA491.S46 2006
  516'.156—dc22   2005032752

© 2007 by Scholastic Inc.
All rights reserved. Published simultaneously in Canada.
Printed in Mexico.

CHILDREN'S PRESS, and ROOKIE READ-ABOUT®,
and associated logos are trademarks and/or registered trademarks
of Scholastic Library Publishing. SCHOLASTIC and associated logos
are trademarks and/or registered trademarks of Scholastic Inc.

1 2 3 4 5 6 7 8 9 10 R 16 15 14 13 12 11 10 09 08 07

9-28-06

3 6879 00067 3694

Would you rather look
at a picture of your
birthday present or
open a real present?

3

A picture of a present is an example of a flat surface. It is a two-dimensional, or 2-D, object.

A real present has many flat surfaces. It is solid, so you can hold it and look at it in different ways. It is a three-dimensional, or 3-D, object. I wonder what is inside of this box?

5

There are names for
the many 3-D shapes
all around us. They are
spheres, cylinders, cones,
rectangular prisms, cubes,
and pyramids.

Can you imagine a
birthday party with 2-D
shapes instead of 3-D
shapes? Do you think
the party would be fun?

Look at the fruit and candy on this birthday party table. Do you see different round 3-D shapes?

These shapes have both curved and flat surfaces.

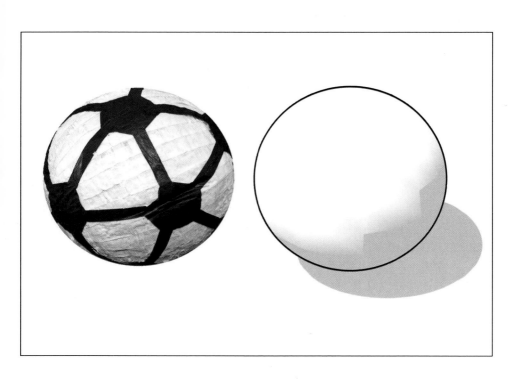

A sphere has a curved
surface. It is round with
no edges, just like a ball.

This piñata is shaped like a sphere, but it probably won't keep its shape for long.

A cylinder has a curved surface and two flat surfaces.

This container is shaped
like a cylinder. Cylinders
are good for storing
party food!

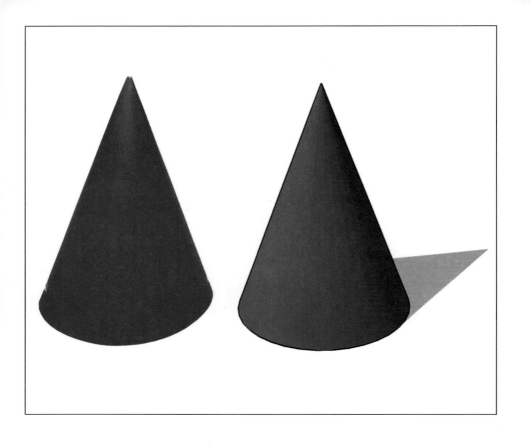

A cone has one curved
surface, one flat surface,
and a point.

A party hat is shaped like a cone. Put one on and join the party!

Spheres, cylinders, and cones are sure to make the party more fun.

faces

There are many 3-D
shapes with straight edges
only. They have flat
surfaces called faces.

They have corners where
the straight edges meet.

corners

A rectangular prism has
four faces and two bases,
like a box.

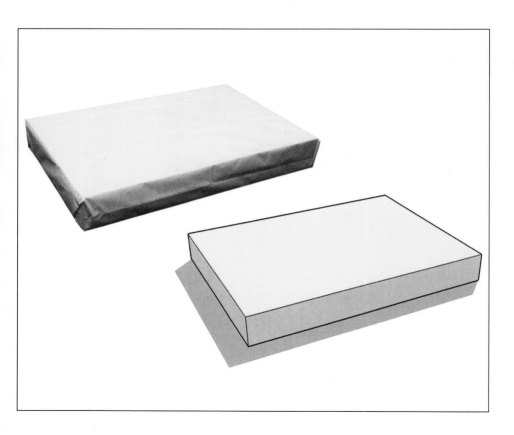

Many people think the
perfect rectangular prism
is a present!

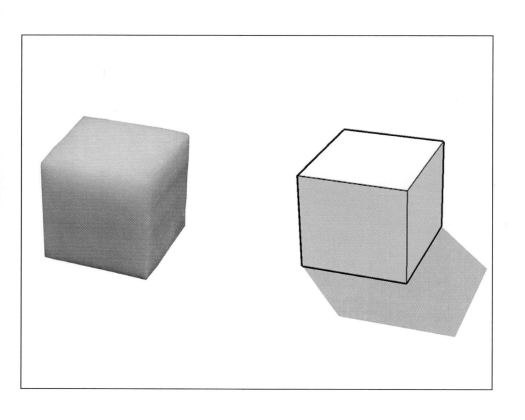

A cube has six faces,
and they are all squares.

Cheese cubes, anyone?

A pyramid has three
or more faces that are
triangles. The triangles
meet at a point.

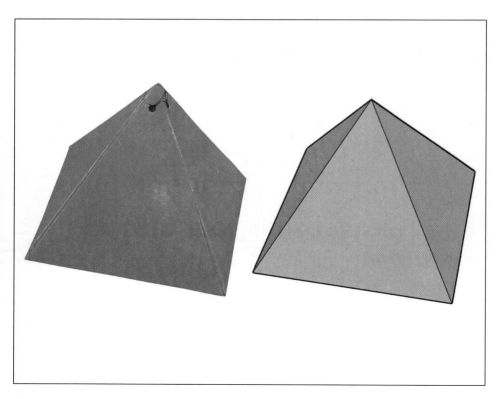

What could be inside
this pyramid?

Look around you.

What 3-D shapes with edges, faces, corners, and bases do you see?

Many different kinds of 3-D shapes can make a party more interesting and fun.

Happy Birthday!

29

Words You Know

cones

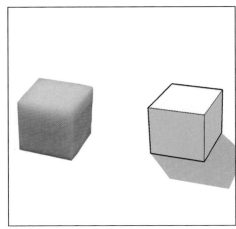

cubes

cylinders

edges

30

faces

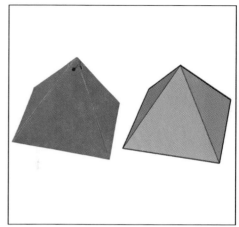

pyramids

rectangular prisms

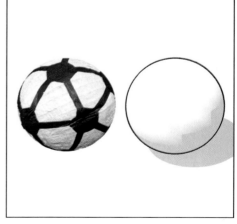

spheres

31

Index

About the Author

Ellen B. Senisi is a writer and photographer. She lives in Schenectady, New York, with her husband, three children, four cameras, and more than fifteen thousand slides and digital photographs. She doesn't get very many presents anymore, so she had fun working on this book.

Photo Credits

All photographs © 2007 Ellen B. Senisi.
Computer renderings by Paul J. Newman.

SUGAR GROVE PUBLIC LIBRARY DISTRICT
54 Snow Street / P.O. Box 1049
Sugar Grove, IL 60554
(630) 466-4686